YOUR KNOWLEDGE HAS VALUE

- We will publish your bachelor's and
  master's thesis, essays and papers

- Your own eBook and book -
  sold worldwide in all relevant shops

- Earn money with each sale

Upload your text at www.GRIN.com
and publish for free

Eddie Fisher

Managing Emotions in Project Environments

How to manage people's feelings at work effectively

GRIN Publishing

Bibliographic information published by the German National Library:

The German National Library lists this publication in the National Bibliography;
detailed bibliographic data are available on the Internet at http://dnb.dnb.de .

Imprint:

Copyright © 2012 GRIN Verlag, Open Publishing GmbH
Print and binding: Books on Demand GmbH, Norderstedt Germany
ISBN: 978-3-656-22375-7

This book at GRIN:

http://www.grin.com/en/e-book/196329/managing-emotions-in-project-environments

"Manage feelings in your projects well, and you are more likely to deliver your projects successfully"

Author: Prof Eddie Fisher

Presented at the ACSA Project Management Seminar in Brno, Czech Republic, June 2012

Abstract

The management of feelings in projects is important. Project managers who recognise this and act accordingly, are more likely to deliver their projects successfully. Managing emotions in projects is of particular importance due to the nature of projects. They are temporary organisations that often consist of a mixture of people from both inside and outside of the organisation. Project managers often do not exercise direct line management responsibility over these so they need to manage the emotions of people over which they have no control.

This variety of human beings such as contractors, vendors and so on, needs emotionally-aware project managers who are 'strong in interpersonal skills, knowing how to create an environment where people feel valued and motivated to contribute to their maximum potential, and where problems are considered challenges and errors are considered learning experiences (Verma, 1996). It is, therefore, essential that project managers in the Project-oriented society become competent in managing the feelings of people well within their projects.

Introduction

I once received an E-mail, by accident, from someone who communicated with a colleague at work. They had a difference of opinion. Emotions were 'flying high'. On closer investigation I found out that they were actually sitting next to each other but only communicating by E-mail. This had been going on for a while.

I knew both so I asked them to share their issue with me. They had a minor misunderstanding but each side was not prepared to give in to move forward. The problem was that of not understanding how the other person felt, accepting these feelings and sharing them with each other. Once I explained to them the importance of sharing feelings with each other, they started to communicate again.

All people have feelings, good or bad. To understand how they feel and why they feel the way they do is important for effective project managers. They have a need to understand and manage the feelings of the team as well as their own to deliver the goals of the project. This can be very challenging at times as it is not easy to manage people.

Honey (1988,1997),Verma (1996) and Goleman (1998) carried out extensive studies on human behaviour during the 1990s. They found that when the emotional side at work is managed well, people feel better about each other and are far more productive.

It is not just this understanding and the application of emotions that could lead to improvements in managing people better. It is also the interrelated association with meeting what others require, building a good personal relationship in a timely manner, talking about and exchanging each other's thoughts, ideas and feelings, and managing emotional conflict well that relate to people's feelings.

Project managers can develop people competences. I will discuss in this paper how this could be achieved, using some real life experiences from projects I have managed and quoting some of the work carried out by recognised experts in this area to support my views.

1.   Emotions in Projects

1.1   Meeting Each Other's Needs

When people have the need for something, they often enter into personal relationships with others so that their needs can be fulfilled. For example, if you want to learn how to snowboard, you develop a relationship with someone who is an expert who will pass on his knowledge to you. Or if you want to know more about collecting stamps, meet a philatelist and ask him questions.

But for this to work, you also need to consider what you can give to these people in return for what they have given you. In order to establish a long-lasting, solid and productive relationship, you need to reciprocate favours. By meeting each other's needs, you are more likely to establish this desired relationship with others (Weisinger, 1998).

This approach is particularly important in project team environments to gain the trust and support of those over whom you do not necessarily exercise any direct line management control. To identify what the needs of others are and how they feel, you have to communicate with them. You have to understand how others feel about themselves , others and the world around them. You need to communicate with people because the spoken word contains details of how people feel. You must also listen carefully to what they have to say. Put yourself in the other person's place. Try to answer the question 'What does he/she really need?' Empathise with people.

Meeting each other's needs is about understanding the wants and needs of others, without making our own judgements or interpretations, based on what we want and need. Emotions often run high in projects because people do not take the time to listen actively to what others have to say.

I recently managed a project with team members from 18 different countries and cultures. One of the countries wanted to launch a new service like the others but could not because of a different technical set-up. I assumed that their machinery was fully compatible with the rest of the countries. This was not the case. I did not ask them what they needed. I assumed all was well. But it was not. I should have empathised with them and asked relevant questions, to find out what they needed. This would have given them the feeling that I really cared about their needs.

I did not make an effort to see things from their perspective, nor did I ask them how they felt about this situation. Instead of putting my needs first (to get the country launched by a given date), I should have identified their needs first, together with the rest of the team, to find a way forward.

Using emotions intelligently means that people understand each other's needs and the reasons why they have these. They can then start to change their behaviours and thinking in order to achieve better results in their projects by recognising the emotional needs people have.

I made a mistake but I learned from it. Developing interpersonal expertise by being emotionally engaged with others is the first step on the long road to become an emotionally intelligent project manager.

1.2   Relating To Each Other Over Time

Developing personal relationships with project team members is important for project managers. These relationships should outlast the project and continue to go on for much longer and provide a good investment not just for a single project.

Over a period of time you need to develop feelings for each other. It is this interchange of feelings that is so important to your relationship with others. I remember when I first met the new project team members of one of my projects at the kick-off meeting in Duesseldorf, Germany in March 2002. Project Managers from six different countries got together, face to face, to deliver a new global product. Everyone felt nervous and uneasy because we did not know what to expect from each other, nor did we have any idea what the other person would be like as a human being.

I took the time to greet and welcome everyone personally, for a few minutes at a time, prior to the start of the meeting. I told them briefly about myself, my background and my role in this project, and what I was hoping to achieve with their inputs and help. Using an appropriate amount of humour, this also helped to 'break the ice'. I shared some of my feelings for the project and the team members with them in an open, honest and direct manner. Some of the project managers started to do the same. They had listened to me, and probably liked what they saw (or at least they could relate to what I had said).

This gradual exchange of niceties as well as business information had the desired effect. We started to build a rapport that was based on our feelings and emotions. For it to work, these had to be authentic and contain details of what was important to us. We created an environment of attachment and affiliation, forming the basis for trust and mutual respect. By letting genuine emotions become part of our conversation, we exchanged authentic feelings with each other, recognising and accepting what was important to each of us (Kets de Fries, 2001).

Being able to share each other's feelings makes all the difference between just being project team members and accepting each other as equal partners in a new joint venture, for example. Project teams will bond that much quicker. It is a much longer-lasting relationship that will be borne out of this, one that can and will, sometimes , last a very long time.

1.3   Exchanging Information Regarding Feelings, Thoughts and Ideas

There is more to building good emotional rapport with project team members than discussed in the previous sections. Effective project leaders will think about how their emotional engagement with team members-through the sharing of thoughts, ideas and feelings-can guide their relationships in a positive direction. The more we experience how to make the best use of these, the more likely it is that the outcome will be positive, and as such, contribute to the success of our projects.

It appears that many behaviours can be associated with positive outcomes. Here are some that project managers should have when managing the emotional side in their projects:

1. If you already feel bad, do not engage in sharing feelings with other people. Your negative thinking will be noticed. It gets in the way of listening actively to what the other person is saying. If you are emotionally disturbed, or perhaps angry, then wait until such a time that you have calmed down. Once you are in a stable frame of mind again, you are more likely to listen to what others have to say, without letting your negative feelings get in the way and affect your judgements.

    Knowing and understanding when not to engage in emotional conversations, is a key behaviour and competence of highly effective project managers.
    People who are or seem to be pre-occupied, will not necessarily give you their full attention. They are otherwise engaged, thinking about something else that occupies their minds. They are emotionally disengaged. They tend not to listen to what you are saying. Because of this, their emotions are unbalanced. They will not be able to tell you what they really think and how they actually feel. There is no value in asking them for their thoughts and ideas and feelings until such a time when they are properly engaged again, for example, in conversations with you.

2. Assess the feelings and moods of project team members first. Then decide how to best proceed with discussing, for example, activities or people issues. It is important to understand what emotional state people are in before engaging them in these discussions. How people feel determines how people work or what attitude they show towards you and the other team members.

    Understanding this helps project managers to decide what topics can be discussed, and how these should be discussed. There is a right time and right place for everything. Project managers need to learn to observe the emotions and feelings of others and then make value judgements what to say and how to say it. They need to assess the likely impact their words/statements will have on people. This will be the difference between failure and success in managing people well.

3. If you notice that those you wish to talk to display negative emotions and feelings, you need to consider what approach to take to turn your discussion into something positive. It is the responsibility of project managers to turn the negative into the positive. Irrespective of any negative tone to the discussion by your project team members, set the scene by being positive in how you come across to the other party. For example, you can draw on positive examples from the past: how well you got on so far, how you respected each other for what you were, and how open and honest you have been to each other in the past.

Reminding yourselves of the good things that you already have in common will help you to get off on a positive note. You are using positive emotions to put the other party in a positive frame of mind. Even if they had negative thoughts and were perhaps even angry, using this approach will facilitate rational discussions. It is all too often that people dwell for too long just on the negative. Positive thinking facilitates positive emotions.

Managers who are emotionally aware of others, will manage the people side better in their projects. Goleman (1998, page 3) refers to this as 'being judged by a new yardstick .'but also by how well we handle ourselves and each other'.

He goes on further by saying that good leaders need to have two abilities to be able to influence the emotional behaviour of others: empathy, which involves reading the feelings of others, and social skills, which allow handling those feelings artfully.

4. It is important to bring out negative feelings or feelings of discomfort. For example, if one of your project team members feels that you are not treating him/her well or that you openly favour someone else to do the 'sexier' jobs within the project, then you must resolve these bad feelings immediately. It is not acceptable to ignore feelings as they will not go away. Based on my extensive experience, they will get worse before they may get any better.

Project managers need to have the ability to be able to discuss feelings of discomfort openly and honestly with people in their projects. Being able to do so means that the true feelings people have about each other can be brought out into the open. This forms the basis for open and honest discussions that lead to more favourable solutions to resolve issues people may have. Project managers need to sense the feelings of others, being aware of their perspectives and taking an active and genuine interest in their concerns.

2.   Moving Towards the Emotionally-competent Project-oriented Society

The Association for Project Management's Body of Knowledge (APM, 2000) under Section 7: People, does not mention 'to manage the emotions of people' as a core competence for project managers. Some of my fellow Ph.D. students at the Open University in the United Kingdom have also suggested that managing emotions in projects is not a competence. I disagree and will argue that it is a competence and give the reasons for saying so.

Project managers must be competent in managing the emotional side of people well within their projects if they wish to achieve their goals successfully. They need to be aware of and understand what it means to manage the emotions within the project team. Goleman (1998) suggests that the feelings of people are ignored, based on research he carried out in the subject matter during the late 1990s. When feelings are ignored, people are not as committed to do things as they could be, they are not highly motivated and they have a tendency not to be genuinely interested in the project.

In the first part of my paper I have already discussed why it is important that project managers manage the emotional side in their projects well. We looked at the necessity to meet each other's needs, to relate to each other over time and the important behaviour of exchanging information about one's feelings, thoughts and ideas.

Competence is about how we do things such as actively listening or managing conflict. In this respect, managing the emotions of others and oneself is no different. It is how we manage relationships with others by understanding their feelings and communicating with them at appropriate levels. Based on the outcomes of my own Ph.D. research-to find new 'managing people' competences to improve the APM's BoK Section 7: People, I have identified a number of behaviours that could form a new competence framework for project managers, such as 'Managing the emotions of people well in Projects'.

People are guided by what and how they feel about things. It is important that these emotions are managed well by project managers so that team members can make informed decisions that are based on solid and unambiguous feelings.

The same is true to say for effective conflict management. Every project has conflicts. It is important that project managers manage these, at the emotional level, to enable them to turn conflicts into something positive so they can move forward. Manage the feelings well in conflicts and you will have the people on your side to deliver work packages successfully. You can deliver better solutions because you have drawn on the knowledge and experience of the team.

Project managers need to encourage team members to share their emotions openly and honestly within the project team environment. The essential words here are 'open' and 'honest'. If people hold feelings back or they do not say exactly what they feel and why they feel it, then it will not be possible for the team to gel or bond. Kets de Fries (2001) calls this behaviour 'authentizotic', as in 'authentic', meaning true or genuine, and 'zotic', meaning what is important to me.

Project managers need to see things from the other person's point of view or perspective, too. There is always more than one way of looking at or seeing things. Take in all views and let people feel that you really value their inputs. Showing empathy means that you are respecting their points of view or perspectives. In return, people will develop trust and respect for you.

Project managers need to manage their own feelings well. They need to understand why they feel the way they do so they can relate this to the feelings of others. They can then use this understanding to turn situations to their benefit. This is particularly useful, for example, when dealing with personal conflicts when emotions are already running high. Defuse the situations by understanding why the other party feels the way they do, then relate this to your own. You are then more likely to find a good compromise and way forward.

Do not get personal in conflicts. Remain rational and business-like. If others attack you at the personal and emotional level, stay in focus and concentrate on the work solutions you need to achieve.

Mayer and Salovey (1997) identified four building blocks that, when developed properly, can dramatically increase people's ability to enhance their emotional competence in projects:

1. The ability to accurately perceive, appraise and express emotion
2. The ability to access or generate feelings on demand when they can facilitate understanding of yourself or another person
3. The ability to understand emotions and the knowledge that derives from them
4. The ability to regulate emotions to promote emotional and intellectual growth

I have discussed a number of behaviours that can be associated with many emotions in your projects. These behaviours are observable events that tell us how project managers 'manage' emotions in their projects. As such, they show us 'how competent' project managers are in this area. Managing emotions is a competence like, for example, managing conflicts. It is about how project managers actually do things. I recommend to accept 'managing emotions' as a new 'managing people' competence in the Project-oriented society.

Conclusions

Project managers need to recognise at the start of their projects whether the team is able to deal with emotions. They must lead their team to identify the emotional reality that exists within the team. For example, does the team find it easy to manage conflict situations or do they prefer to shy away from them?

Teams need to recognise what feelings constitute the 'belonging to the team'. This is the job of the project manager. It is at this point that project managers must instil the emotional side within their projects. And why teams first and not the individual? Goleman, Boyatzis and McKee (2002) argue that it is for motivational reasons that this is so. As individuals we are motivated when we have access to our dreams and to our own vision of the future. It provides us with the energy we need in order to change our behaviour. This is difficult in teams. The vision is often in the far distance and does not give the team enough short-term motivation to change their behaviours.

Teams need to understand their emotional reality at the emotional level. For example, why is it that they do not harmonise as a team or why they feel uncomfortable to resolve conflicts? Teams often change their behaviour only after they have recognised their emotional reality.

Project managers need to effectively share their perceptions of another person's feelings. They need to make it clear that the perceptions are theirs, not someone else's. Their body language needs to show, for example, that they really are actively listening to what the other person is saying, accepting what is being said. They must avoid challenging statements such as 'You do not know what you are doing'. Instead, they need to use neutral statements that do not make the other party go into defence. A better way of saying the same thing is perhaps 'You usually work very well but your excellent standard has dropped recently. Why is this?'

Perceptions can be deceptive, particularly when they have been misinterpreted. It is important that project managers check that their perceptions are valid. They need to check regularly with the other party that they have understood their feelings correctly. It is important to state to people that the perceptions are yours and not someone else's. For example, if they think that someone feels angry, they should ask 'I feel that you are feeling angry. Is this correct?'.

Accept what the other person is saying and make sure that your body language follows this. Do not in any way suggest that you are making a negative suggestion. Do not use a language that may appear to be challenging to the other party. For example, instead of using statements such as "You still do not understand", use phrases such as "It looks as if I am confusing you".

Check regularly with the other party whether you are picking up their feelings correctly. For example, " I can feel that you are feeling disappointed. Is this correct?" Being aware of your feelings and behaviour as well as perceptions others have of you, could influence your actions in such a way that they could work to your benefit.

Being aware of the feelings people have at all emotional levels within your project is a key project management competence. Imagine what it would be like to work with project teams where everyone communicates with understanding and respect, where people help each other willingly to achieve their goals and where people enjoy working because they are able to express their feelings openly and honestly. Project managers in the Project-oriented society could be the catalyst for making it happen within their organisations.

References

Goleman,D.(1998).*Working With Emotional Intelligence*, Bloomsbury Publishing Plc.

Goleman,D.;Boyatzis,R. and McKee, A.(2002). Emotionale Fuehrung, Econ

Honey,P.(1988, 1997).*Improve Your People Skills*, Second Edition, Chartered Institute of Personnel and Development

Kets de Fries,M.F.R.(2001).*Creating authentizotic organisations: Well-functioning individuals in vibrant companies*, Human Relations, Volume 54, Number 1, January 2001, pages 101-111

Mayer, J.D. and Salovey,P.(1997)."*What Is Emotional Intelligence?*" In P. Salovey and D.Sluyter(eds.),*Emotional Development and Emotional Intelligence: Implications for Educators*, New York: Basic Books

Verma,V.K.(1996).*Human Resource Skills For The Project Manager-The Human Aspects Of Project Management*, Volume Two, Project Management Institute

Weisinger,H.(1998).*Emotional Intelligence at Work*, Jossey-Bass

2 Different Approaches for the ethical dilemma of non-forcible Humanitarian Interventions

To show the different viewpoint in the discussion I further highlight the two most contradictory approaches: The Utilitarian and the Kantian one.

2.1 Utilitarian Approach

Utilitarianism is a subfield of the Consequentialism, which justify actions for maximal goodness of the majority and for the value of the final consequence (Brink, 1986). The happiness of the majority is normally in the focus of Utilitarian viewpoints. Heinze (2006) replaces ´happiness` by ´security` to adapt this to the issue of H.I. Security is a major and vital goal for states. Hence –from this viewpoint- states are allowed to intervene, when the security is in danger. In case of non- military interventions we could mention the case of SARS or other epidemics. Here the intervention with e.g. border controls, NGOs monitoring the situation in the country, treating people, vaccinate people against governments` permission, etc. would be allowed. On the other hand, if security for the majority can´t be achieved by this, intervention is not necessary (Heinze, 2006). An example here is the cross-border intervention from MSF in Afghanistan in the 80´s- MSF came undercover in the country to treat people in rural areas, etc. (Raich, 2002). The consequence here doesn´t prove advantage for the security of the majority and is hence not permitted. Slim (2002) describes even, that H.I. can increase harm. In the case of the above mentioned example this becomes clear, because when this intervention gets known by the government or other groups in the country, this could increase the danger for conflict in international relations or could bring the MSF-workers into danger. Another Utilitarian point is, that sovereignty of states is important to respect. Mill (1859), who is often quoted by many authors, describes this right of states as elementary and explains further, that people should be allowed to live in liberty without any intervention of other states. In liberty means also, that they have the chance to demonstrate against their government, to act self-determent in their county, like it has happened in many countries before. Mill calls this the ´tyranny of the majority`, which can lead to positive results within the borders of countries. With this point of view the Utilitarian argue, that an Intervention is only legitimate in an extreme case of violations of Human Rights (Heinze, 2003). Walzer agrees to this approach by adding, that an H.I. is only justified, if governments

lose their legitimacy by violating strictly against their own populations´ rights (Heinze, 200[
about Walzer).

2.1.1 Critics to the Utilitarian approach

The first critic, that mostly appears in this context of H.I. is, that the value of human rights o
individuals is totally underestimated by the Utilitarianism. This means, that we act only whe
aggregate human suffering is existing. Further this raises the question, when the point o
action begins. When exactly is the point, where the majority benefits. We can even be not 10(
percent sure, whether this is the case, because we can only suggest what the consequence
would be- but we don´t know for sure. On the one hand we can overestimate the situation an
react and this could result in harm, war or other negative effects for the majority. On the othe
hand we could underestimate the situation, don´t react and e.g. an epidemic could be
unavoidable (Heinze, 2003). The second point of critic rises in the argument of states` rights
Of course states have the rights to be sovereign and thereby to enjoy the principle of non
intervention. But does the right count more than the rights of individuals in the states, whos
rights are violated (Mertens, 2004)?

2.2 Kantian Approach

The Kantian approach belongs to the deontological viewpoints, which propose, that killing o
violating the rights of others is never justifiable and hence we have the ´categorical` -or in thi
case- ´humanitarian imperative` to intervene. This means, that we have the duty to interven
in cases, where our moral understanding tells us to act. We can´t be blamed for something w
do due to this humanitarian reasons- no matter which consequences it has in the end (Driver
1997; Slim, 2002). With regard to the cross- border interventions of MSF in Afghanistan, th
Kantian approach would clearly support this intervention, although maybe more helpers die o
are injured than people benefit from the intervention (Holmes, 1990).

Holmes (1990) interprets the analysis of Tèson (1988), who claims, that human rights don´
end at national borders. If they are violated it is our duty to intervene. He even claims, tha

wars are just, when they are for human rights. The non-consensual, but also non-forcible H.I. are insofar legitimated, too. Miklos (2009) adds, that states are only sovereign and hence no intervention takes place, when they respect human rights of their own population. The rights of humans are universal and independent of nationality. Here it is also important to mention, that conflicts between different civil- groups are not left out as a requirement for intervention. If the state is not able or willing to protect the human rights of parts of their population, which are violated by other parts of the population, then H.I. is legitimated, too (Heinze, 2003). This non- intervention –by ability or willing of the state- is also a form of intervention and hence a clear decision against the protection of human rights (Raich, 2002).

Further, the Kantian approach would agree to the Utilitarian approach to intervene in situations, like the rising danger of an epidemic, e.g. SARS- but they have got different arguments. The Kantian approach wouldn´t react to save the majority´s life, but for the reason of protecting any violation of human rights (security and health in this example). In an actual case the methods would be different. The Kantian approach would also mean to protect the human rights of already infected. Those are innocent and have the right to get all necessary health supply. Utilitarian would be more strict with isolating those people and focus on the healthy majority (Miklos, 2009).

2.2.1 Critics to the Kantian approach

The Kantian argumentation is currently often used by the NGOs , which claim to work for human rights and to have the duty to intervene. In deed this view has been new in the 70´s, when Bernhard Kouchner was one of the founders of MSF. The Biafra – in Nigeria- was the reason for building the NGO. The state didn´t allow the UN or the ICRC[2] to come into the country to deliver the basic supply for the people suffering from war. The organizations respect this prohibition due to the principle of non- intervention. MSF has the goal to react in all cases, where human rights are violated, although the states don´t agree to this intervention (Redfield, 2005). This NGO is a symbol for the Kantian approach and hence also often attacked by critics. The main critic is here, that those H.I., which are mainly lead by the humanitarian imperative, are often not structured and the results are consequently poor (Slim,

---

[2] ICRC: International Committee of the Red Cross

2002). The most cited example is here the case of Rwanda, 1994, where some NGOs wer
into the country (Rwanda's government entrusted them not to do), where almost one millio
people were killed in a genocide, to build camps and to give medical and physical assistanc
to those, who survived. Actually, they brought many resources in a country, where a war too
place. Those resources were often the aim of rebels. Consequently they supported the wron
and brought themselves and the refugees even more into trouble (Rieff, 1997). In this way th
main critic is according the most important ethical principle of "do not harm" (Anderson
1996). Driver (1997) adds, that harm can be a result of non-forcible H.I. even if it is we
planned and NGOs are careful; Who is then responsible for this harm? We have got not onl
a moral responsibility to intervene, but also a causal responsibility with regard to th
consequences of an H.I. He claims, that it is sometimes morally problematic to intervene, i
you think about the consequences. Stewart (1998) agrees by giving the number of 30 millio
refugees, who suffer worldwide from refugee- related trauma, which could be often avoide
by NGOs.

The second main argument from opponents of the Kantian approach is the fact, that thi
behavior reminds of colonization. It would be in so far a form of humanitarian neo
colonization in contrast to the former territorial form (Slim, 2002). It is not in general
problem to go into other countries for helping, but it is a moral issue to go in such countrie
without the express request of the government and with the values and methods of th
"western world". Bell and Carens (2004) give an example of Mogadishu, where people woul
rather die than to lose one of their limbs. This is a highly problematic situation for helpers
who were there to save lives and couldn´t combine the actual situation with their own value
and knowledge. Those naturally try to convince people to get medical treatment, but where i
the border between an advice to do something and an urge?

A more practical argument comes from Rieff (1997) and Atack (1999), who both emphasiz
on the importance of the relationship between NGOs and states. An intervention in th
absence of political solution solves hence nothing. The relation between both actors consist
of conflict, competition, cooperation and cooptation. And naturally NGO prefer to work wit
democratic states. But nevertheless a consensual way must be found with all other states on a
international/ macro-level. Otherwise the micro-level interventions of NGO will come t
nothing than conflict.

Conclusion

One basic point, which seems to be the first obstacle in the analysis of this topic is the fact that there is no consensus about what H.I. exactly is about and where the borders are to Humanitarian Aid, Humanitarian Assistance, Humanitarian Operations and further the distinction forcible, non, forcible and non- consensual interventions. A profound discussion about the topic is highly aggravated by this (Raich, 2002).

The discussion of the ethical dilemmas showed first, that a dispute with this topic is unpreventable and second, that beside the differences in both approaches some parallels can be found:

The topic is unpreventable, because the work of NGOs is about lives and they can bring lives even into danger as we heard about the critics from the Kantian approach. Furthermore it is unpreventable, because the number of NGOs increases more and more. The question is who gets which money and how are all resources in the end allocated. There should be clear understandings for what the money is used. Further people donate with the vision of long-term and efficient help (Rieff, 1997). But is it morally right to use this money e.g. for unofficial non- consensual cross- border interventions in Afghanistan?

Secondly, there are –although hidden- some parallels between the approaches. I would suggest to start here for addressing this dilemma. Although NGOs, like MSF, work in the name of deontology, they have learned from mistakes in the past. It is not their plan to go unprepared in a country- regardless of all risks. H.I. are planned, many helpers are experienced and well educated. A disaster like in Rwanda 1994 shouldn´t happen again. This is something where both approaches agree (Rieff, 1997; Raich, 2004).

In general more attention must be paid to NGOs work. They command a great fortune with money, technical equipment, educated staff and of course experience. There is no governing position about NGOs; the structures are connected loosely between different NGOs. An open discourse and a critical evaluation is necessary in the global framework of states and organizations about the role and legitimacies –the ethical dilemmas- of the NGOs and in particular also about their non-consensual interventions. The topic has too long been in the background behind the discussion of the legitimacy of military interventions. But the fact, that

we don´t see the unofficial interventions so obvious doesn´t mean, that they are not happenin
and have the potential to produce harm or to use valuable resources ineffective.

List of Literature

Anderson, M. (1996) Humanitarian NGOs in Conflict Interventions [online] In: *Managing Global Chaos.* pp.343-354. Available online: [active: June, the 12th 2010].

Attack, I. (1999) Four Criteria of Development NGO legitimacy. *World Development* 27 (5), pp.855-864.

Bell, D.A. and Carens, J.H. (2004) *Human Rights Quarterly* 26 (2), pp. 300-329.

Brink, D.O. (1986) Utilitarian Morality and the Personal Point of View. *The Journal of Philosophy.* 83 (8), pp. 418,419.

Driver, J. (1997) The ethics of Intervention. *Philosophy and Phenomenological Research* 57 (4), pp.851-870.

Heinze, E.A. (2003) Waging War for Human Rights: Toward a Moral-Legal Theory of Humanitarian Intervention [online]. *Human Rights and Human Welfare* 3 (2003), pp. 83-94. Available online: http://www.du.edu/korbel/hrhw/volumes/2003/heinze-2003.pdf [active: June, the 6th. 2010].

Heinze, E.A. (2006) Maximizing Human Security: A Utilitarian Argument for Humanitarian

Intervention [online]. *Journal of Human Rights* 5(3), pp. 283-302. Available online: http://www.informaworld.com/smpp/content~content=a756770110&db=all [active: June, the 6th. 2010].

Holmes, R.L. (1990) Review: Humanitarian Intervention: An Inquiry into Law and Morality *Law and Philosophy* 9 (3), pp.319-323.

Mill, J.S. (1859) *On Liberty.* [online]. Ontario, Batoche Books. Available online: http://socserv.socsci.mcmaster.ca/oldecon/ugcm/3ll3/mill/liberty.pdf [active: June, the 6th. 2010].

Mills, K. (2005) Neo- Humanitarianism: The Role of International Humanitarian Norma and Organizations in Contemporary Conflict [online]. *Global Governance* 11, pp.161-183. Available online: http://homepage.mac.com/vicfalls/isa2002.pdf [active: June, the 14th 2010]

Mertens, T. (2004) Humanitarian Intervention: Legal and Moral Aguements *In:* Meggle, G. (eds.) *Ethics of Humanitarian Interventions*. Heusenstamm, ontos verlag. PP.215-230.

Miklos, A. (2009) Public Health and the Rights of States. *Public Health Ethics* 2 (2), pp. 158 170.

Raich, J. (2002) Ethical Evolution of the Humanitarian Idea [online]. Barcelona, Medicines sans frontiers. Available online: http://www.jordi-raich.com/Articulos/AA18-Evolucion.pdf [active: June, the 6th. 2010].

Redfield P. (2005) Doctors, Borders, and Life in Crisis. *Cultural Anthropology,* 20 (3), pp.328- 361.

Rieff, D. (1997) Charity on Rampage: The Business of Foreign Aid. *Foreign Affairs,* 76 (1), pp. 132- 139.

Slim, H. (2002) Claiming a Humanitarian Imperative: NGOs and the Cultivation of Humanitarian Duty [online]. *Refugee Survey Quarterly* 21 (3), pp.113- 125. Available online http://rsq.oxfordjournals.org/cgi/reprint/21/3/113.pdf [active: June, the 12th 2010].

Stewart, D.E. (1998) Human Rights Issues and Health Practices. *Asia- Pacific Journal of Public Health* 10 (94), pp.94-99.

Wheeler, N.J. (2004) *Humanitarian Intervention after 9/11*[online]. Aberystwyth, University of Wales. Available online: http://cadair.aber.ac.uk/dspace/bitstream/2160/1939/1/Humanitarian%20Intervention%2c %20Wheeler.pdf [active: June. The 6th. 2010].